P9-DHM-380

≡ *The Godfather Doctrine* draws essential lessons from perhaps the greatest Hollywood movie ever made to illustrate America's changing geopolitical predicament. In it, John Hulsman and Wess Mitchell show how the aging godfather, Don Vito Corleone, is emblematic of Cold War American power on the decline in a new and dangerous world, and how the Don's heirs uncannily exemplify the three leading schools of American foreign policy today. Tom, the left-of-center liberal institutionalist, thinks the old rules still apply and that negotiation is the answer. Sonny is the Bush-era neocon who shoots first and asks questions later, proving an easy target for his enemies. Only Michael, the realist, has a sure feel for the changing scene, recognizing the need for flexible combinations of soft and hard power to keep the family strong and maintain its influence and security. Expanding on Hulsman and Mitchell's widely debated article, "Pax Corleone," *The Godfather Doctrine* explains for everyone why Francis Ford Coppola's epic story holds key insights for ensuring America's survival in the twenty-first century. ≡

John C. Hulsman and A. Wess Mitchell

The Godfather Doctrine ≋

A FOREIGN POLICY PARABLE

PRINCETON UNIVERSITY PRESS

PRINCETON AND OXFORD

Published by Princeton University Press, 41 William Street,
Princeton, New Jersey 08540
In the United Kingdom: Princeton University Press, 6 Oxford
Street, Woodstock, Oxfordshire OX20 1TW

Library of Congress Cataloging-in-Publication Data

Hulsman, John C., 1967–

    The Godfather doctrine : a foreign policy parable / John C.
Hulsman and A. Wess Mitchell.

        p. cm.

    ISBN 978-0-691-14147-3 (hardcover : alk. paper)   1. United
States—Foreign relations—1989–   2. Godfather films—History
and criticism.   I. Mitchell, A. Wess, 1977–   II. Title.

    JZ1480.H85 2009

    327.73—dc22

                                                2008042881

British Library Cataloging-in-Publication Data is available

This book has been composed in Minion Pro
Printed on acid-free paper. ∞
press.princeton.edu
Printed in the United States of America
10 9 8 7 6 5 4 3 2 1

To Eva and Elizabeth,
the ultimate wartime consiglieres

Contents ≋

The Godfather Doctrine

"The Don, rest in peace, was slippin'.

Ten years ago could I have gotten to him?"

  —Virgil "the Turk" Sollozzo

Introduction ≊

The age of American global dominance is
drawing to a rapid and definitive close. In
the space of barely a decade, the United
States has slipped from a position of seemingly inexhaustible national strength to one
of breathtaking vulnerability. Crowning
its victory in the Cold War, the American
Republic sat atop an economic, diplomatic

and military power base rivaling that of the Roman Empire. American businesses set the pace of global commerce; American diplomats piloted international institutions whose rules we ourselves had written; and American armies were underwriters of peace in the world's remotest regions. America's was a power so irresistible, and an influence so pervasive, that no country, large or small, could reasonably hope to succeed in an international undertaking without Washington's blessing.

That world is gone. America in 2009 is economically palsied, diplomatically isolated, and militarily exhausted. Rather than a triumphant stroll along the flagstone-paved pathway to a new American Century, the country's current course looks more and more like a grim and unforgiving trudge down the steep and rocky slope of decline. Upon assuming office, the forty-fourth president will inherit two simultaneous land wars, a rapidly arming Iran, a brooding and reanimated international jihad, a tottering atomic Pakistan, a $500 billion budget deficit, a devastating mortgage and investment banking crisis, a $700 billion bailout of the financial sector, and the weakest dollar in modern American history. He will also be the first U.S. president since the end of the Cold War to face a world in which America must share its seat in the global cockpit with other Great Powers. A resurgent and energy-rich Russia, a geopolitically awakened India, and a booming and proud China—all see themselves as rising powers gaining traction at the expense of the United States. They will expect to have a say in how the world is run.

Just as the challenges facing the United States are growing more numerous, the tools for managing them will be scarcer than ever. With a national image still deeply disfigured around the world by the Iraq War and a Western alliance system on the verge of rupture, the next president could well find himself commander-in-chief of the loneliest nation on earth.

This is not the America that emerged victorious from the life-or-death struggle of the Cold War. Chastened and confused, America must find the courage, resources, and, above all, creativity to navigate a world unlike anything that U.S. statesmen in living memory have had to confront. For we live in a world none of us studied in school. It will neither be wholly dominated by one great empire nor be the chessboard on which many countries with roughly equal power vie to establish their dominance. We are entering new geopolitical territory. For a long time, the United States will remain chairman of the global board of directors. But it is not enough merely to look to America anymore. The confusing thing will be that there are new and rapidly growing board members, and that the board's membership will vary depending on the issue. Brazil will be new to the board, as will China. Gone is the comforting simplicity of the old Cold War era, with one enemy to fight, one ideology to defeat, one opposing system to understand. Ours is a strange and complicated new world.

To survive and prosper in this radically transformed age, America's leaders, we believe, must adopt a radically new strategy—one that is fundamentally different, in its core assumptions and preferred instruments, from the alternatives currently posed by either of the nation's two major political parties. Like most Americans, we believe that the "neoconservative" approach to foreign policy that has held sway in Washington for the past eight years has been disastrous and must be discarded. But we also believe that the intellectual alternative put forward by the Democratic Party—"liberal institutionalism"—will also leave the nation ill-prepared for the epochal change that lies ahead.

Instead, we believe that, in a time of unprecedented crisis, the United States must employ the least ideological and most thoroughly tested approach to foreign policy at its disposal—a school of thought known as "realism." At its root, realism can be reduced to a simple proposition: that, in order to anticipate and adapt to change in international politics, you must first understand the nature, uses, and limitations of power, tailoring strategies to the actual capabilities a country possesses. In this, it differs from its intellectual competitors, both of which—despite their seeming partisan animosity—share a preoccupation with how other states are governed on the inside. If only foreign governments could be brought—through force of arms or force of diplomacy—to resemble our own, so the reasoning goes, America could finally and definitively inoculate itself, and the rest of the world, against the old contagions of war, crisis, and geopolitical competition. History could then come to an end as the rest of the globe would look like America, sharing both its values and its interests.

This is a laudable dream, as dreams go. But it is well beyond the current power of the United States, or indeed any power in recorded history, to accomplish. The pursuit of such an unrealistic dream will soon morph into the unending nightmare of national decline as the rest of the world, not convinced that it should give up its ambitions to follow an arrogant America, fights back militarily, economically, and diplomatically. Saying that we mean well is unlikely to convince the rest of the world to forsake its own dreams, values, and interests.

Such a gargantuan undertaking would have been beyond America even during its heyday following 1945. In the new multipolar era, it should be comical to think the United States need merely dictate, and others will follow. But such a view is still all too popular in both parties. This is because both neoconservatism and liberal institutionalism—much as their adherents often personally dislike one another—share an understandable vice, that of nostalgia for a world that has passed them by. It is entirely human to want to continue to live in the simple Cold War world, where America was dominant, its choices clear, its strategy set. As a result, America increasingly finds itself with a unipolar mind-set and a bipolar toolbox in a multipolar world. When this dangerous affection for a past that cannot be re-created in today's changed world is linked with universalist policy goals that no great power could ever hope to enact, the end result is a great acceleration in

America's decline. For realists are surely right that, to make the world better, we must see it as it is, warts and all, rather than as we would like it to be.

Yet despite the increasingly obvious inadequacies of its competitors, realism has not taken the American foreign policy community by storm. With their hopeful outlook, refusal to retreat from even the largest of world problems, and principled stand on the merits of democracy, the Democratic and Republican iterations of the "Wilsonian" approach to foreign policy—be it through liberal institutionalism or through neoconservatism—are widely thought to be quintessentially American, and have prospered. It is as if people would rather be demonstrably wrong, but well-meaning, than adopt a point of view that may be right but seems cold, bloodless, and plodding. By contrast, realism—with its laser-like focus on assessing power relationships and the often discomforting insights this brings—conjures up images of Old World European cynicism. It is gloomy, unsexy—in a word, un-American. America, so the thinking goes, is not suited to playing power politics: realpolitik is simply not in our political DNA. As a result, Wilsonian foreign policy strategies have gained a near monopoly among the nation's decision-makers—a monopoly that is likely to dominate the next four years just as it did the previous eight.

This is more than unfortunate. It is dangerous. For we believe that realism has something unique to say about America's growing predicament in world affairs—something that the other schools, for all their boundless optimism, are not equipped to provide us. Far from an antiquated, foreign transplant, realism as a concept is in fact deeply rooted in the American national consciousness—not only at the top, but in the collective popular imagination. To specifically protect America and its people above all other considerations so they can get on with enjoying the personal benefits of liberty that come from living in a strong, prosperous, powerful country; to believe that too much power in the hands of any one group (or country) has the potential to corrupt and should therefore be balanced; to deny that any government, including our own, has all the answers for what ails the world—all are uniquely American insights that inform modern realism as well.

Instead of being foreign, realism has been a large part of the American discourse since the administration of George Washington and the signing of the Jay Treaty with our then enemy Great Britain. Washington and Alexander Hamilton made it clear that securing peace for the American people should supersede distaste for doing a deal with the formerly hated George III. This hardheaded approach set the fledgling American Republic on its way to its eventual rendezvous with destiny, as the essential modern great power confronting the horrors of both Hitler and Stalin. Contrary to the arguments of realism's foes, Americans have in many ways been realists from the founding. That has been one of the secrets of our success.

That is precisely why it is such a pity, from our point of view, that the pragmatism so inherent both in realism and in American foreign policymaking since the founding has been submerged (but not eliminated) by the recent dominance of the liberal institutionalist and neoconservative schools of thought, which start from utopian premises, not being based upon a practical assessment of the world we actually find ourselves in. The founders would know better.

But if realism's critics are wrong in saying that it is un-American, they are right that it is unsexy: In recent years, realists have shown little interest in making their insights understandable to the American public. Too often they have gloried in their craft as if the world were merely a mathematical formula that needed working out, one that should be explained only to an inner-circle priesthood of true believers who had enough intellect and guts to see the world as it truly was. To put it mildly, such elitist nonsense is not likely to lead to political success in any democratic country. Realism has come to resemble the worst kind of Shakespearean production, glorifying in the bard's obscurity, forgetting that the secret to his universal appeal is that he wrote the plays using themes and language that everyone of his day could entirely understand. Realism, like Shakespeare, must be for everyone.

We strongly believe that realism, beyond the usual academic cloisters, needs to reconnect with the people of this country, if it is to remain relevant. To make this point, and to convey what we believe is a message of grave importance for the future of the American Republic, we have chosen an unconventional format for this book. Precisely because the stakes for the United States are now so high and our current policymaking habits so predictably tragic, we—both of whom are prolific foreign policy analysts—believe we cannot afford to simply add another book to the growing list of foreign policy analyses that are being written to advise the next president.

Instead, we have chosen to present an allegory of American power drawn from that most American of mediums—film—and that most American of film dramas: Francis Ford Coppola's *The Godfather*.

The idea of using this iconic 1972 movie to explain U.S. foreign policy was born in Berlin's Kreuzberg district, a most un-Mediterranean setting, on a November night in 2007. While we had independently realized the film's parallels to the world of geopolitics, it was not until Wess joined John for a *Hefeweizen* one night at his Berlin apartment that we realized the movie's full potential to convey the seriousness of America's current predicament and the strategic alternatives that are available for handling it. For in his chronicling of the rise, fall, and rebirth of the Corleone Mafia empire, Coppola presents two hauntingly prophetic messages that speak directly to America today: that the fall of the powerful is inevitable; and that we have options for how we respond to this tragic truth, make the most of the hidden opportunities it presents, and chart a course to renewed strength.

The travails of the Corleone family in the anarchic and fluid world of organized crime are not unlike those America will face in the anarchic and fluid world of geopolitics. Like Coppola's characters, America today can rest assured that adjustment will come; it is simply a question of on whose terms. And while Americans may not be a cynical people, we are—like the Corleones—a practical people, a people who value their birthright enough to make hard decisions in hard times, outwitting intelligent foes to prosper in a world cut loose from the moorings of everything we thought—and hoped—it would be.

And so we present a parable of American statecraft, offered at a moment of unexampled danger, in the hopes that our

Republic will foresee the coming earthquake, and prosper in spite of it. We present *The Godfather Doctrine*.

John C. Hulsman
Berlin, Germany

A. Wess Mitchell
Washington, DC

June 15, 2008

The Godfather Doctrine ≋

*The Godfather and
American Foreign Policy*

The Don, alone, walks across the street
to pick some fruit from the stand. He
mumbles pleasantly to the Chinese owner,
then turns his skilled attention to the task.
However, his peaceful idyll is shattered by

the sounds of running feet and multiple gunshots. Vito Corleone, head of the most powerful of New York's organized crime families, lies slumped over his car, with five bullet holes in his body.

Virgil "the Turk" Sollozzo arranged the hit on Vito, as the Don refused to ally with him in expanding into the very lucrative narcotics trade. By a miracle, he is not dead, only gravely wounded. His three sons, Santino (Sonny), Tom Hagen, and Michael, gather in an atmosphere of shock and panic to try to decide what to do next, with the towering figure of the Don looming over them all. For the Godfather was more than just the most successful mafioso of his era; he has come to epitomize a power structure that has stood the test of time. All that has been imperiled, along with the Don's dwindling life.

This, of course, is the hinge of Francis Ford Coppola's *The Godfather,* one of the greatest movies ever produced by American cinema. *The Godfather* has always been a joy to watch; however, given the present changes in the world's power structure, the movie becomes a startlingly useful metaphor for the strategic problems of our times. The aging Vito Corleone, emblematic of Cold War American power, is struck down suddenly and violently by forces he did not expect and does not understand, much as America was on September 11th. Even more intriguingly, each of his three sons embraces a very different vision of how the family should move forward following this wrenching moment. The sons approximate the three American foreign policy schools of thought—liberal institutionalism, neoconservatism, and realism—vying for control in today's disarranged world order. While we certainly accept that analogies have their limits, taking a fresh look at *The Godfather,* and the positions of the three quarreling sons, casts an illuminating spotlight on the American foreign policy debates that rage today.

The Consigliere

As Vito's three sons gather, the future of the Corleone dynasty hangs in the balance. The first brother the family turns to for advice is Tom Hagen, the German-Irish transplant

who serves as "consigliere" (chief legal adviser) to the clan. Though an adopted son, Tom is the most familiar of the three brothers with the inner workings of the New York crime world. As family lawyer and diplomat, he is responsible for navigating the complex network of street alliances, backroom treaties, and political favors that surround and sustain the family empire. His view of the Sollozzo threat and how the family should respond to it is an outgrowth of a legal-diplomatic worldview that shares a number of philosophical similarities with the liberal institutionalism dominating the foreign policy outlook of today's Democratic Party.

Liberal institutionalism found its modern prophet in Woodrow Wilson, the vainglorious president who pledged fighting a war

to end war itself. Along with this messianic disregard for history as it has been lived, its key features include a core conviction that rules can be used to trump power, and a corresponding predilection for using international institutions to tackle global problems. But liberal institutionalism goes beyond this, seeing such organizations as the United Nations as being endowed with a unique global legitimacy, as if the institutions themselves were the critical players on the chessboard, with states playing an important but secondary role. As such, nations must give up a significant portion of their sovereignty in order to endow such clubs with power. In a similar way, Tom believes that by relinquishing their individual freedom of maneuver and seeking consensus at the meetings of the Five

Families (a kind of UN Security Council), local Mafia clans can cast off their thuggish beginnings and replace the rough-and-tumble world of gangland geopolitics with a cooperative framework for jointly governing the streets of New York.

It is with this larger goal in mind that he assesses the Sollozzo threat. Like many modern Democrats, Tom believes that the family's main objective should be to return as quickly as possible to the world as it existed before the attack. His overriding strategic aim is the one that Hillary Clinton had in mind when she wrote in a recent *Foreign Affairs* article of the need for America to "reclaim our proper place in the world." The "proper place" Tom wants to reclaim is a mirror image of the one that American politicians remember from the 1990s and dream of restoring after 2008. Like pre–September 11th America, the empire that Vito built in the years leading up to the Sollozzo attack was a "benign hegemon"—a sole Mafia superpower that ruled not by conquest, but by institutions and strategic restraint.

This is the system that Tom, in his role as consigliere, was responsible for maintaining. By sharing access to the policemen, judges, and senators that (as Sollozzo puts it) the Don "carries in his pocket like so many nickels and dimes," the family managed to create a kind of Sicilian Bretton Woods—a system of political and economic public goods that benefited not only the Corleones, but the entire Mafia community. This willingness to let the other crime syndicates "drink from the well" of Corleone political influence rendered the Don's disproportionate accumulation of power more palatable to the other families, who were less inclined to form a countervailing coalition against it. The result was a consensual, rules-based order that offered many of the same benefits—low transaction costs of rule, less likelihood of great-power war, and the chance to make money under an institutional umbrella—that America enjoyed during the Cold War.

It is this "Pax Corleone" that Sollozzo, in Tom's eyes, must not be allowed to disrupt. In dealing with the new challenger, however, Tom believes that the brothers must be careful not to do anything that would damage the family business. The way to handle Sollozzo, he judges, is not through force but through negotiation—a second trait linking him to today's liberal institutionalists. Like more than one of the recent Democratic contenders for the presidency, Tom thinks that even a rogue power like Sollozzo can be brought to terms, if only the family will take the time to hear his proposals and accommodate his needs.

Throughout the movie, Tom's motto is "we oughta talk to 'em"—a slogan that, in the period since the publication of the National Intelligence Estimate (NIE) report on Iran, has begun to harden into ortho-doxy among the lawmakers and presidential hopefuls of the Democratic Party, who now say that immediate, unconditional talks with America's latest "Sollozzo"—Mahmoud Ahmadinejad—is the only option still open to Washington for coping with the Iranian nuclear crisis.

The party's growing veneration of diplomacy as the sine qua non of American statecraft rests, as it did for Tom, on two assumptions: (a) that, despite their aggressive posturing, the Sollozzos of the world would rather be status quo than revolutionary powers, and (b) that the other big families have a vested interest in sustaining the Pax Corleone and will therefore not use the family's distraction with Sollozzo as an opportunity to make their own power grabs. Working from these assumptions, today's consiglieres have prescribed the same course of action regarding Iran that Tom prescribed for dealing with Sollozzo: a process of intensified, reward-laden negotiation (what Senate Majority Leader Harry Reid calls a "diplomatic surge") that they believe will pave the way for his admission as a normalized player into the family's rules-based community.

This near-religious belief in the efficacy of diplomacy brings Tom into bitter conflict with those in the family, led by Sonny, who favor a military response to Sollozzo. To Tom, as to many Democrats, Sonny's reveling in the family muscle runs counter to the logic of institutionalized restraint that Vito used to build the family empire. In the world that Tom knows, force is used judiciously and as a last resort: only on the rarest of occasions, and after repeated attempts at negotiation, would the Don dispatch Luca Brazi to cajole and threaten an opponent—"To make them an offer they can't refuse"—and even then, it was usually with the foreknowledge and multilateral consent of the other families. By contrast, the street war Sonny launches against Sollozzo is an act of reckless unilateralism—a Mafia equivalent of the Iraq War that, unless ended, threatens to upset Tom's finely tuned institutional order and squander the hard-won gains of the Pax Corleone.

At first blush, Tom's critique of Sonny's militarist strategy sounds reasonable. Compared with the eldest son's promiscuous expenditures of Corleone blood, treasure, and clout, Tom's workmanlike emphasis on consensus building has much to recommend it; if successful, it would permit the Corleones to resume their peaceful hegemony to their own and the other families' benefit.

But the hope Tom offers the family is a false one. For in order to be successful, the consigliere's diplomacy must be conducted from a position of unparalleled strength, which the family no longer possesses. In this sense, he is more like Sonny than he realizes; despite the seemingly vast philosophical differences between them, each wields an instrument of policy that was forged in a bygone age: for Sonny, the ability to field "a hundred buttonmen" at a moment's notice; for Tom, the luxury of always being the man at the table with the most leverage. But the era of easy Corleone dominance is over. Though neither brother realizes it, power on the streets has already begun to shift into the hands of the Tattaglias and Barzinis—the Mafia equivalent of today's "BRICs" (Brazil, Russia, India, and China). Like the current international system, the situation that confronts the

Corleone family is one of increasing multipolarity—a reality that is lost on Tom, who thinks he is still the emissary of the dominant superpower (a delusion that many Democrats apparently share).

But even if Tom doesn't know the world is shifting, Sollozzo does. Like the two-bit petty tyrants who challenge Washington with mounting confidence in today's world, Sollozzo senses that fundamental changes are under way in the global system, and knows that they give him greater latitude for defying the Corleones than he had in the past. As Sollozzo tells Tom, "The Don, rest in peace, was slippin'. Ten years ago could I have gotten to him?" The consigliere is wrong about Sollozzo. He is not, like challengers in the past, out to join the Pax Corleone. He is an opportunist who will take things as they come—as either a revolutionary power or a status quo power, but certainly as one out to accelerate and profit from the transition to multipolarity. The other families have no more incentive to thwart his maneuvers than Russia and China have to thwart those of Iran. And because Tom fails to see this, his strategy is the wrong one for the family, and the wrong one for America.

Shoot First and Ask Questions Later

Sonny, the Don's undisputed heir, is the most shaken by the attempted hit on his father, whom he venerates. His simplistic response to the crisis is to advocate "tough-ness" through military action, a one-note policy prescription for waging righteous war against the rest of the ungrateful Mafia world.

Disdaining Tom's pleas that business will suffer, Sonny's damn-the-torpedoes approach belies a deep-seated fear that the only way to reestablish the family's dominance is to eradicate all possible future threats to it, however remote. While such a strategy makes emotional sense following the attempted hit on his father, it runs counter to the long-term interests of the family. Vito himself knew that threats against his position were a fact of life; while his policy revolved around minimizing them, he well knew that, in a world governed by power, they could never be entirely eliminated. As the Don put it to Michael, "Men cannot afford to be careless."

By contrast, Sonny's neoconservative approach is built around the strategically reckless notion that risk can be eliminated from life altogether through the relentless—and if necessary, preemptive—use of violence.

In Sonny, Tom is confronted with the cinematic archetype of the modern-day neoconservative hard-liner. Their resulting feud resembles the pitched political warfare between Democrats and neoconservatives that has come to dominate the American political landscape:

NEOCON: "Hey get this, Sollozzo wants to talk—can you imagine the nerve on that son of a bitch? Last night he makes a hit on pop, today he wants to talk . . ."

LIBERAL INSTITUTIONALIST: "We oughta hear what they have to say."

NEOCON: "No, no more. Not this time, Consigliere; no more meetings, no more discussions, no more Sollozzo tricks."

LIBERAL INSTITUTIONALIST: "Sonny, this is business, not personal."

NEOCON: "Well then business will have to suffer, alright? And do me a favor: no more advice on how to patch things up—just help me win alright?"

Where Tom sees Sollozzo as a reasonable if aggressive businessman whose concerns, like those of previous challengers, can be accommodated through compromise and conciliation, Sonny sees an existential threat—a clear and present danger that, like Iran in the view of many Republicans, must be swiftly cauterized.

One can imagine that Sonny's shoot-first-and-ask-questions-later approach would meet with the firm approval of arch-neoconservatives such as Norman Podhoretz and Michael Ledeen. Confronted with the Iran crisis, Sonny would urge an immediate military strike, primarily as a way to cut through ambiguities and arrive at some sort of moral and strategic clarity, however illusory. As with the neoconservatives, so desperate to remove a possible emerging nuclear threat from Iran, it is unlikely that Sonny would make a cost-benefit analysis of such a military strike.

What, the Iranian leadership has checks and balances, and Ahmadinejad is not even in control of Tehran's nuclear program?

Don't waste time, says Sonny. A U.S. air strike would fail to accomplish anything of lasting military value and would only succeed in uniting Iran (and the region) against America? Stop being weak, says Sonny. A failed strike would imperil American allies in the region, such as in Pakistan, Saudi Arabia, Jordan, Morocco, and Egypt, directly benefiting al-Qaeda? I knew you didn't have the guts to do this, says Sonny. As is true for neoconservatives, Sonny would be unlikely to let facts get in the way of his desire for military action, however wrongheaded.

Instead, by starting a gangland free-for-all in the wake of the hit on his father, Sonny unwittingly severs long-standing family alliances and unites much of the rest of the Mafia world against the Corleones.

The resulting war, like America's Iraq debacle, is one of choice rather than strategic necessity. As has been true with empires since the beginning of time, Sonny's rash instinct to use military power to solve his structural problems merely hastens the family's decline.

As the past few years have shown, military intervention for its own sake, without a corresponding political plan, leads only to disaster. Yearning for the moral clarity that the Corleones' past dominance had given them—a dominance not dissimilar to that enjoyed by America during the Cold War—Sonny cannot begin to comprehend that the era that made his military strategy possible has come to an end. Blinded by a militant moralism bereft of strategic insight, he proves an easy target for his foes.

The neoconservatism that Sonny espouses grew out of a movement that has been far less prominent in American history than either Tom's liberal institutionalism or Michael's realism. Emananting from disillusioned Trotskyites, such as Irving Kristol, who had belatedly seen the error of their ways in Stalin's excesses, these fierce Cold Warriors have remained true to a core principle of their earlier allegiance—permanent revolution, this time for a democratic world.

As Trotsky said of socialism, only when the whole world hewed firmly to a single ideological line could the planet be genuinely safe for sustained peace and prosperity. Modern-day neocons, substituting democracy for socialism, have arrived at the same conclusion, evidenced by President

Bush's second inaugural address declaring that America cannot really be secure while tyranny exists in the world. The problem with this view is that such an end of history does not correspond with any period in the global record. It is a formula for perennial warfare, living beyond the country's means, and a quick decline for America, still the greatest hope of the world.

Sonny's fate is emblematic of neoconservatism's follies. Unwisely, and against the advice of his mother, Sonny attempts to arbitrate the escalating domestic disputes between his sister, Connie, and her abusive husband, Carlo Ricci, failing to see that the beatings his sister endured from Carlo came at the behest of Don Barzini, the Corleones' closest peer competitor. For Sonny's reaction to all the evils of the world, whether beyond his ability to solve or not, is entirely predictable: "Attack." Unilaterally rushing to avenge his sister by pummeling Carlo, Sonny is struck down by his legion of foes, his body riddled with bullets. As has proven true for the neoconservatives over Iraq, there is a depressing logic to his hit. In place of understanding the world, Sonny based his strategy on accosting it; the world's striking back, as happened in Iraq, is an obvious conclusion.

The Realist

The strategy that ultimately saves the Corleone family from the Sollozzo threat and equips it for coping with multipolarity does not come from either of the brothers who dominate family war councils at the beginning of the movie, but from Michael, the youngest and least experienced of the Don's sons. Unlike Tom, whose labors as family lawyer have produced an exaggerated devotion to negotiation, and Sonny, whose position as untested heir apparent has produced a zeal for utilizing the family arsenal, Michael has no formulaic fixation on a particular policy instrument. Instead, his overriding goal is to protect the family's interests and save it from impending ruin by any and all means necessary. In today's foreign policy terminology, Michael is a realist.

Viewing the world through untinted lenses, he sees that the age of dominance the family enjoyed for so long under his father is ending. Alone among the three brothers, Michael senses that a shift is under way on the streets toward a more diffuse power arrangement, in which multiple power centers will jockey for position and influence. To survive and succeed in this new environment, Michael knows the family will have to adapt; the policy instruments it relied on before will have to be recalibrated. Unlike Tom, whose grand strategic vision centers on the concept of restoration, and Sonny, whose strategy is about retribution, Michael sees the time has come for wholesale strategic retrenchment. Three characteristics of his strategy allow it to succeed where the others fail, and could provide a blueprint for reinventing U.S. foreign policy today.

First, Michael relinquishes the mechanistic, one-trick-pony policy approaches of his brothers in favor of a "toolbox" in which soft and hard power are used in flexible combinations and as circumstances dictate. Like realists today, he knows that the family must cut the coat of its foreign policy according to the cloth of its material power base. While at various times he sides with Tom (favoring negotiation) or Sonny (favoring force), Michael understands their positions to be about tactics, and not about ultimate strategy, which for him is solely to ensure the survival and prosperity of the family. Thus he is able to use Sonny's "buttonmen" to knock out those competitors he cannot co-opt, while negotiating with the rest as Tom would like. This blending of sticks and carrots ensures that Michael is ultimately a more effective diplomat than Tom and a more successful warrior than Sonny: when he enters negotiations, it is always in the wake of a fresh battlefield victory and therefore from a position of strength; when he embarks on a new military campaign, it is always in pursuit of a specific goal that can be consolidated afterwards diplomatically.

Applied to America's current predicament with Iran, Michael's strategy would call for a carefully timed mixture of both carrots and sticks to dissuade Iran's leadership from producing nuclear weapons. Carrots would include foreign investment, American diplomatic recognition, fora to discuss and address outstanding U.S.-Iran issues, and a nonintervention pledge from the United States. Sticks would include the prospect of an international investment freeze that would quickly bring the Islamic Republic to its economic knees.

While realists accept that, in the end, the leadership in Tehran will decide the course it takes, such a flexible approach prepares America for whatever Iran ultimately decides to do, and changes the odds of Iran's acquiring nukes, while leaving the United States at the head of a considerable coalition of other powers.

This is a policy approach that realists have been advocating for years and which has been largely ignored. The neoconservative/Sonny approach has already been chronicled. The Democrats, for their part, are equally scornful of the realist prescriptions. For all their talk about "keeping all options on the table," in reality the strategies that Clinton and Obama have in mind involve mostly carrots—neither is prepared to use sticks to prevent Tehran from obtaining nuclear weapons. Dennis Kucinich, though strictly a fringe candidate, spoke for the majority of Democrats when he warned the two lead candidates that any "threatening statements and actions against Iran" would be viewed as "naïve and fool-hardy" by the party base. Nor are Democrats likely to bring serious nonmilitary inducements to bear; like most EU countries—most notably, Germany—they fear that an economic freeze on Tehran would backfire, allowing China to capture Persian markets and provoking continued Russian opposition in the United Nations. Until Washington abandons these inhibitions, it is unlikely to be taken any more seriously by Iran than Tom was by Sollozzo.

Second, Michael understands that, no matter how strong its military or how savvy its diplomats, the Corleone family will not succeed in the multipolar environment ahead unless it learns to take better care of its allies. Like America after the Iraq War, the Mafia empire that Michael inherits after the hit on Sonny is characterized by a system of alliances on the brink of collapse. Having flocked to the Corleone colors when the war against Sollozzo broke out, the family's allies—like America's in the "New" Europe—have little to show for the risks they have undertaken on the family's behalf. Exhausted by war and estranged by Sonny's Rumsfeld-like bullying, they have begun to question whether it is still in their interests to backstop a declining superpower that is apparently not interested in retaining their loyalty.

For all his talk about diplomacy, Tom believes in the family's dominance; like today's liberal institutionalists, he assumes that allies will continue to pay fealty to the family as a matter of course, as they have in the past. Similarly, Sonny assumes that other powers will gravitate toward the family or risk irrelevance; like most neocons, he sees allies as essentially disposable. By contrast, Michael intuitively grasps the value of family friends and the role that reciprocity plays in retaining their support for future crises. Thus he is seen offering encouragement and a cigarette to Enzo, the timid neighborhood baker whose help he enlisted, like Poland in Iraq, to protect his father at the hospital. In this, he is imitating his father, Vito, who saw alliances as the true foundation of Corleone power and was mindful of the need to tend the family's "base" of support, not only with big players like Clemenza and Tessio (Britain and France) but with small players like the cakemaker and undertaker (Bulgaria and Romania) whose loyalty he is seen cultivating in the opening scenes of the movie.

For as Michael knows, even small allies could potentially prove crucial in "tipping the scales" to the family's advantage, as they will for America, once multipolarity is in full swing. Relearning the lost Sicilian art of alliance management will be necessary if Washington is to regain the confidence of the growing list of allies whose loyalty was frittered away, with little or nothing to show in return, in the sands of Iraq.

In advocating his realist course for the family, Michael is drinking deeply from the well of American geopolitical experience. True to realist form, his concerns are not some esoteric apocalyptic goal, such as the rise of global institutions bringing about everlasting peace or striving to live in a tyranny-free world; rather the welfare and the continued prosperity of his very tangible family are the object of all his efforts. Likewise for realists, the welfare of actual Americans now inhabiting an actual America is the focal point of all their endeavors. Instead of believing in a utopian and blissful future that none of us will see, Michael's realist vocation turns his efforts toward the protection and betterment of genuine people, rather than abstractions.

Conclusion: Creating a New Order

Third, while addressing the family's immediate need for a more versatile policy tool kit and shoring up its teetering alliances, Michael also takes steps to adjust the institutional playing field to the Corleones' advantage on a more fundamental, long-term basis. Where Tom sees institutions as essentially static edifices that act as a source of power in their own right, and Sonny sees them as needless hindrances to be bypassed, Michael sees institutions for what they truly are: conduits of influence that "reflect and ratify" but do not supplant deeper power realities. When the distribution of power shifts, institutions are sure to follow. As the Tattaglias and Barzinis gain strength, Michael knows they will eventually overturn the existing order and replace it with an institutional rule book that better reflects their own needs and interests. Evidence that this process is already under way can be seen in the ease with which Sollozzo is able to enlist the support of a local precinct captain—the Mafia equivalent of a UN mandate—when police loyalties formerly belonged to the Corleones. Similarly, Washington increasingly finds the very institutions it created after World War II being used against it by today's rising powers, even as new structures are being built (like the Shanghai Cooperation Organization) that exclude the United States as a participant altogether.

Rather than ignoring this phenomenon, as Tom does, or, like Sonny, launching a frontal assault against it, Michael sees it as a hidden opportunity. For Michael knows that if the family will act decisively, before the Tattaglias and Barzinis have acquired a commanding margin of power, it can rearrange the existing institutional setup in ways that satisfy the new power centers but still serve vital Corleone interests. This he does through a combination of accommodation (dropping the family's resistance to narcotics and granting the other families access to the Corleones' coveted New York political machinery) and institutional retrenchment (shifting the family business to Nevada and giving the other families a stake in the Corleones' new moneymaker, Las Vegas gambling). In this way, he is able to give would-be rivals renewed incentives to bandwagon with, rather than balance against, the Corleone empire, while forcing them to deal with Michael on his own terms.

A similar technique could prove very useful for America in anticipating and preparing the way for the emergence of its Tattaglias and Barzinis, the BRICs. In the years ahead, Washington should pursue, as a matter of overriding strategic priority, the renovation and expansion of the Bretton Woods system as a first step toward incorporating the BRICs into a rules-based American world. Such an effort at preemptive institutional regrouping, with decision making predicated on new global power realities, is vital if America's new peer competitors are to eschew the temptation to position themselves as revolutionary powers in the new system. Doing so now, while the transition from the old system to multipolarity is still under way and before the wet cement of the new order has hardened, could help to ensure that, while it no longer enjoys the privileged status of hegemon, America is able to position itself, like the Corleones, as the next best thing: *primus inter pares*—"first among equals." Such an approach will require Washington to emulate Michael's cool, dispassionate courage in the face of epochal change and to avoid living in the comforting embrace of the past, as both Tom and Sonny ultimately did. For in the end Michael's strategic goal is that of America—to preserve its position in a dangerous world.

Epilogue: Critics and Crisis ≋

We have been gratified by the overwhelming reaction our essay has sparked, both
from lovers of *The Godfather* and from fel-
low foreign policy experts. Since its initial
publication in the *National Interest,* versions
of the article have appeared in the *Los Angeles Times* and *Harper's Magazine,* provoking discussion on the editors' blogs at both

the *Weekly Standard* (Sonny territory) and the *New Republic* (Tom territory). And in a demonstration of the universal appeal of Coppola's film—and the universal applicability of realism—the article has been widely disseminated abroad, with translations in several languages. People seem to have competed with one another to stretch our analogy to its breaking point, while displaying an almost encyclopedic knowledge of a film we thought we knew back to front. For the intellectual stimulation and just plain good fun that this has brought us, we would like to thank you.

The first criticism of our parable comes from some foreign policy specialists, uneasy with the lack of grounding our story has in contemporary academic studies of International Relations theory. We fear the above sentence will have our more general readers reaching to close this book. But our specialist colleagues have raised an important point, if not the one they intended to.

For, as we stated in the introduction, the purpose of using a parable is to convey, in succinct form and to a primarily nonacademic audience, the story of American geopolitical decline and the competing policy options that are now available for dealing with that reality. This book is about looking at the worldviews of decision-makers. It was never intended as an academic treatise or primer on International Relations theory.

Far from it. As we have spelled out, one of the primary reasons for writing this book was to get away from the inaccessible postulates of theory and connect with a mass audience around the very different idea of looking at the worldviews of those who directly guide the future course of the country. We both come from this more practical policy-driven world. It is what we do with our day, what we are constantly writing about, and what the general public is far more interested in.

However, this quibble is not what has disturbed most readers; instead they rightly worry about how the end of the movie jibes with what we have laid out in such detail. One main criticism has been tabled. If Michael is such a cautious and measured realist, readers ask, then why does he unleash a torrent of violence at the end of the movie, wiping out the family's enemies? Isn't this something Sonny would do?

Indeed, at first glance, this argument makes sense. We must stress again that our analogy, like all others, has limits. But in terms of the critical factors of timing and objectives, Michael's seemingly explosive mowing-down of his rivals at the end of the *Godfather* films is undertaken for realist reasons, using realist tactics.

First, his objectives are more limited and therefore more achievable than Sonny's. For Michael, in trying to preserve the family, represents a status quo and not revolutionary power. He is not trying, as Sonny is, to return to the simpler, more intellectually satisfying time of family dominance. Rather, he is trying to manage, as America should, a very new world, with very different circumstances.

His rampage is not unrestrained. He is not trying to eradicate the other families as Sonny is; Michael would not approve of neoconservative efforts at regime change. On the contrary, he is trying to deal from a position of strength with his rising peer competitors in the new world in which he finds himself.

Using the realist tools that have been around since the time of Athens, diplomatic carrots and sticks, Michael whacks several of the leaders of the other families to maneuver these rising powers into a more malleable position. By inducing them with the carrot of personal profit, the opportunity to share in the Corleone family's heightened prosperity in Las Vegas gambling, Michael is following tactics of which Tom Hagen would surely approve. But a family policy, or a foreign policy, of merely using carrots suffices only in a world dominated by rabbits.

As Michael knows, along with Sonny, there is far bigger jungle game out there. Force has always been, and will always be, part of the diplomatic equation. It should come as no surprise that the *Iliad*, the West's first great work of literature, is about the universality of war. Michael has ingested this tragic reality with his mother's milk. The other families must be shown that as there is a financial reward that goes with siding with the Corleone family in this new world, so there is a painful penalty for trying to upend the new system by attempting to eradicate Michael's family. It is a lesson not likely to be lost on the new leaders of the rising families, who through Michael's skillful use of carrots and sticks are likely to prove far more amenable to coexisting in this new world, where

Corleone power is still a major factor in Mafia life.

The other major difference between Michael's use of force and Sonny's is timing. Where his elder brother envisions an open-ended feud, during which he will vanquish any and all challengers emerging to contest the family's old dominance, Michael's preference is for a onetime, comprehensive settling of accounts, after which the new system can settle into a stable—and peaceful—period of equilibrium.

Before his plan of strategic retrenchment (the shift to Las Vegas gambling) is set in motion, Michael knows that immediate challenges must first be effectively dealt with. Otherwise, no matter how brilliant his plans out West, the family will be hobbled by lingering wounds from the previous era, as the other families—as yet unconvinced of Michael's ability to fill his father's shoes—use perennial tests of strength to gauge the unfolding power structure.

By devoting all the resources he has inherited from the world that Vito built—all the family's remaining allies, its clout, and, yes, its muscle—to removing the constraints on his *immediate* freedom of maneuver, he is able to pave the way for the Vegas plan to succeed, creating a springboard from which the family can sally into the new era from a position of unmistakable strength.

In a similar way, American policymakers must act decisively now to prepare the way for multipolarity. For if either Michael or America waits too long, steering by the comforting lights of a bygone era, their chance to set the terms for the new world in which they find themselves will be lost. Michael, unlike his older brother Sonny, is not striking out in blind rage. He is acting to preserve the family's position, before his power in the new era drains away. So, too, must America confront the immediate, existential threats it faces—two ongoing wars and the arming of Iran—using the whole of its diplomatic toolbox, so that it can get on with the bigger business of constructing post–Bretton Woods institutions that reflect the genuine power realities of the new multipolar era.

This is a bolder claim than it may at first sound. It has become required writing in almost any work concerned with international relations over the past fifty years to say that we live in a time of crisis, that America finds itself at a turning point, and that a new course must be set. But it must also be remembered that just because the boy cried wolf before, does not mean there is not one now howling at the door.

For we have not yet had our "Truman moment," when the moderate forces around Truman's administration set a policy—containment—favoring political competition with the Soviet Union, which was then adopted by the opposing Republican Party under Eisenhower. Both a left-wing challenge from Henry Wallace, who favored appeasing Stalin, and a right-wing challenge from General MacArthur, who favored rollback of communist states (the regime change of its day) and nuclear war over Korea, were seen off. As this vital center held, America was set for victory in the Cold War.

Such geopolitical creativity has been sadly lacking in the post–Cold War era. The closest thing to intellectual consensus has come from an unholy alliance of liberal institutionalists and neoconservatives. While both tribes often personally dislike each other, as is the case with Tom and Sonny, they strangely share a nostalgic view of the world. While neocons still believe America can politically change other people's hearts and minds with overwhelming military force, liberal institutionalists think that using the right words with today's rising powers, finding the right mantra for negotiating with them, will magically do away with all rising power interests standing in the way of peaceful coexistence with the United States.

Tom Hagen's heirs may feel they went to better universities than did Sonny's adherents; but they do not question that the overall model is one of unparalleled American strength. They are both living in a world that simply no longer exists, yet their policy prescriptions have not remotely begun to catch up to the changing realities of multipolarity.

The recent Georgia crisis illuminates the depressing sameness characterizing both political parties. Georgia's government, despite repeated American warnings, attempted to wrest back control of the Russian-dominated separatist enclave of South Ossetia by force. Russia, overjoyed at this strategic blunder by its enemy, counterattacked Georgia proper, crushing the American-trained army and threatening the capital city of Tblisi.

The responses of the two presidential candidates provided a clear demonstration of how deeply both parties remain mired in the unipolarist mind-set.

Barack Obama, echoing Tom's liberal institutionalist view, argues that, all geopolitical facts to the contrary, Georgia should be admitted into the North Atlantic Treaty Organization (NATO), the preeminent Western military organization, thus rewarding Tblisi for its rashness. This is due to the liberal institutionalist desire to "fill in" the missing pieces of Europe, to achieve the institutional dream, through universal NATO membership, of a "Europe whole and free," underwritten by this most successful military alliance. Such a view disregards the fact that Georgia is utterly indefensible: short of using nuclear weapons, America cannot come to its aid militarily, saving it from the onslaught of a Russian advance. It is to be hoped that America would not accept a nuclear conflagration as the price for "rescuing" Tblisi from Russian dominance.

Incredibly, John McCain, surrounded by neoconservative advisers such as Robert Kagan and supporters such as Bill Kristol, echoes this line, but in bellicose tones reminiscent of Sonny, saying that Russian aggression in Georgia must not stand, as though America stood in wait to militarily repel the Russian army.

In truth, neither school of thought has a practical policy answer for how the two candidates' ambitious rhetoric can be translated into reality. America, hamstrung by a trillion-dollar financial system bailout, and with its armed forces worn bare by grinding wars in Iraq and Afghanistan, simply does not have the manpower or the money to make good on these fanciful boasts.

Worse, realists worry what such a feel-good approach could mean for NATO, which is founded on its Article V commitment that an attack on any of the allies is an attack on all the allies, in line with the three musketeer call of "all for one, and one for all." Ignoring the reality that tiny, weak, and, yes, provocative Georgia sits next to its giant neighbor Russia and far from the core of Europe, America's Toms and Sonnys are trying to write geopolitical checks that the United States simply cannot cash. While realists do not see NATO as an independent power, they do see it as a power multiplier for the United States, a tool to maximize

American strength through the ingrained habit of working with other countries to pursue the common interest of collective security. If NATO takes in members that cannot be defended, it will devalue the security commitment made over the past fifty years to its European allies, discrediting a significant source of American power. For that critical reason, realists resist majority calls in both parties to take in Georgia, whatever the consequences.

But realists, following Michael's belief in avoiding conflict through quiet strength, would also draw clear lines with Putin's Russia, moving troops and basing eastwards into NATO territory in Central and Eastern Europe. This would make it clear to the Kremlin that new NATO member states— such as Poland, Estonia, and Romania—will be protected in line with the standard Article V guarantee. Only by establishing firm boundaries with great power Russia—whose help, by the way, is needed by America on issues as far afield as fighting al-Qaeda, global energy policy, and Iran—can an armed conflict be averted, one that would be as catastrophic as it is avoidable.

Such are the complexities of the new era; tragically, so far reaching back for the comforting if outdated dreams of Sonny and Tom has proved far more intellectually satisfying for both parties. This is worse than fanciful; it is entirely dangerous. The emerging Tom-Sonny consensus, formed around nostalgia for Vito's dying world, is the surest route to speeding American decline. But, as for the family, there remains a clear way out. For if we are right, policy prescriptions emanating from the Sonnys and Toms of this world are bound to continue to fail, as fruit is spoiled that comes from a poisoned tree.

Be the issue alliance management or dealing with rising nondemocratic states such as China and Russia, or newly assertive nationalistic democracies, such as India and Brazil, simply either telling them what to do nicely or threatening them is unlikely to meet with success. But Michael would know what to do. By engaging such states, by looking at their genuine interests, the United States can make accommodations that pave the way for a more stable, more decent world. The carrot of capitalism, which all the rising powers embrace, and the stick of commonly dealing with an al-Qaeda that rejects all states as well as the current system, is a good place to start to look for broader agreements. Only by working with the rising powers over decades can America, at the edges, change their leaders' calculations in our direction, making them stakeholders in an American-inspired international system. This is backbreaking, arduous work, but as Michael might say, "This is the business we have chosen." Surely our children also deserve such foresight.

And that is the issue over which our *Godfather* parable finally breaks down. For America has always been morally worth infinitely more than a Mafia empire. Where Michael goes wrong is not in advocating realism, but in seeing it as a primary virtue—as a worldview that can be applied to the affairs, not just of his business, but also of his family. For America to regain and maintain its glorious lineage as a "City upon a Hill," an inspiration to the rest of the world because of what it stands for as much as for what it does, realism must always remain a secondary virtue. It is an instrument of state, to be brought to bear in the service of the Republic, to safeguard the things about this country—our inspiring history, durable constitutional system, class mobility, economic dynamism, love and use of individual liberty—that brought the Corleones and millions of other families to America to begin with. There is so much in America worth preserving, both for ourselves, our future, and for the world. Realism allows us to preserve all that we hold dear, perpetuate it, and successfully navigate a new era, just as our forefathers did.

Franklin Roosevelt was right in saying that America had a rendezvous with destiny. With a little help from the unlikely wisdom of Michael Corleone, realism will see to it that we will continue to keep that essential appointment.

About the Authors ≋

John C. Hulsman is President and Co-founder of John C. Hulsman Enterprises (www.john-hulsman.com), a successful international relations consulting firm. Hulsman is also the Alfred von Oppenheim Scholar in Residence at the German Council on Foreign Relations in Berlin, a contributing editor to the *National Interest*, and a member of the Council on Foreign Relations. In his career, Hulsman has given more than 1,300 interviews (for outlets such as CNN, CBS, ABC, and Fox), written more than 180 articles (for outlets such as the *Financial Times*, the *Los Angeles Times*, *Harper's Magazine*, and the *National Interest*), and given more than 1,000 briefings to senior policy decision-makers around the globe.

A. Wess Mitchell is Co-Founder and Director of Research at the Center for European Policy Analysis, a Washington, DC–based foreign policy institute dedicated to the study of Central Europe. The author of numerous publications, Mitchell is a frequent contributor to leading U.S. and European newspapers and journals, where his articles and interviews have been translated into more than a dozen languages. In 2005, at the age of just twenty-seven, Mitchell co-founded the Center for European Policy Analysis, which has gained wide recognition as one of Washington's most innovative policy institutes.